Searchlight
BOOKS™

Cutting-Edge STEM

Cutting-Edge Medicine

T0386258

Buffy Silverman

Lerner Publications ◆ Minneapolis

For Jon Silverman, my bionic brother

Lerner Publications Company
An imprint of Lerner Publishing Group, Inc.
241 First Avenue North
Minneapolis, MN 55401 USA

For reading levels and more information, look up this title at www.lernerbooks.com.

Main body text set in Adrianna Regular.
Typeface provided by Chank.

Library of Congress Cataloging-in-Publication Data

Names: Silverman, Buffy, author.
Title: Cutting-edge medicine / Buffy Silverman.
Description: Minneapolis : Lerner Publications, [2020] | Series: Searchlight books. Cutting-edge STEM | Audience: Ages 8–11. | Audience: Grades 4 to 6. | Includes bibliographical references and index.
Identifiers: LCCN 2019011156 (print) | LCCN 2019012411 (ebook) | ISBN 9781541583443 (eb pdf) | ISBN 9781541576810 (lb : alk. paper)
Subjects: LCSH: Medical innovations—Juvenile literature. | Medical technology—Juvenile literature. | Medicine—Forecasting—Juvenile literature.
Classification: LCC RA418.5.M4 (ebook) | LCC RA418.5.M4 S575 2019 (print) | DDC 610—dc23

LC record available at https://lccn.loc.gov/2019011156

Manufactured in the United States of America
1-46663-47659-8/16/2019

Contents

Chapter 1

WHAT IS A MEDICAL BREAKTHROUGH?

Your robot greets you by name when you sit down for breakfast. It gives you your morning vitamin. When it sees your sister, it gives her the allergy pill she needs.

Does this sound like science fiction? It's not! Robots are one of the new technologies helping people stay healthy.

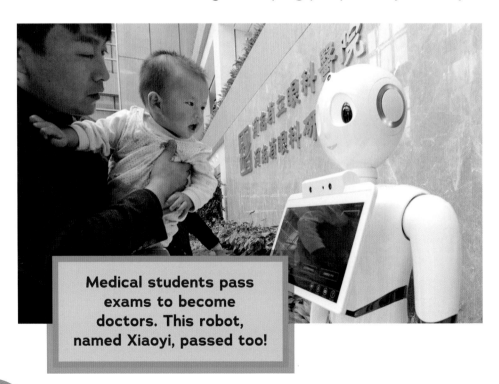

Medical students pass exams to become doctors. This robot, named Xiaoyi, passed too!

A lot of research goes into what doctors tell their patients.

How do you manage your health? A doctor might tell you to exercise and eat nutritious foods. But sometimes it takes more than that to stay healthy. Medical scientists and doctors study how to prevent illnesses. They also research ways to cure or manage diseases. They use new technologies, such as smart robots and 3D printers, to help their patients. These breakthroughs help doctors diagnose patients and provide better treatments.

Robots to the Rescue

Imagine having a robot care for you when you are sick. Another robot might help you get around when you can't move on your own. More and more, robots can help us track and manage our health.

A Japanese robot called Robear looks like a friendly bear. Robear can help patients be more independent. When Robear hears a command, it gently lifts patients out of bed. Using its mechanical arms, it places them safely in a wheelchair. Then they can go where they want without asking for help.

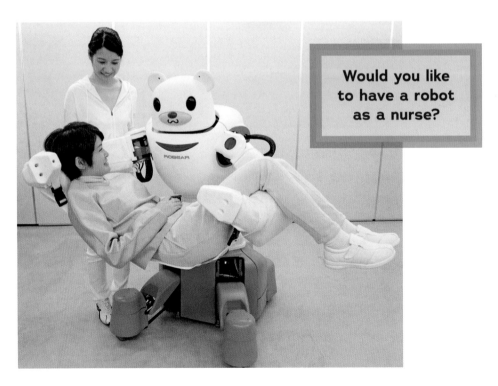

Would you like to have a robot as a nurse?

PILLO CAN TELL PATIENTS WHEN THEY NEED TO REFILL THEIR PRESCRIPTIONS.

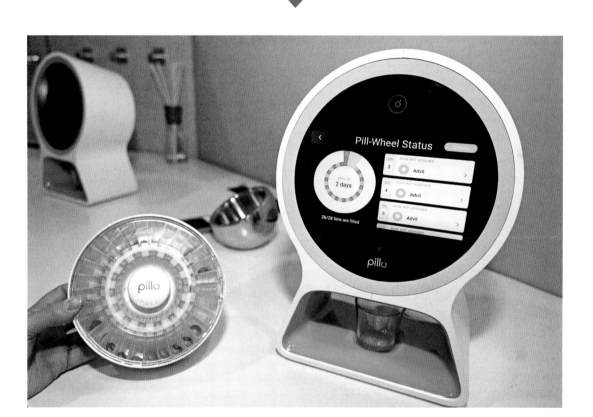

A robot called Pillo reminds patients to take medicines they need. The robot learns to recognize people's faces. Then it gives them their pills at the right time. It will call a nurse or a family member if patients forget to take their pills. Patients can even ask this robot what the weather's like!

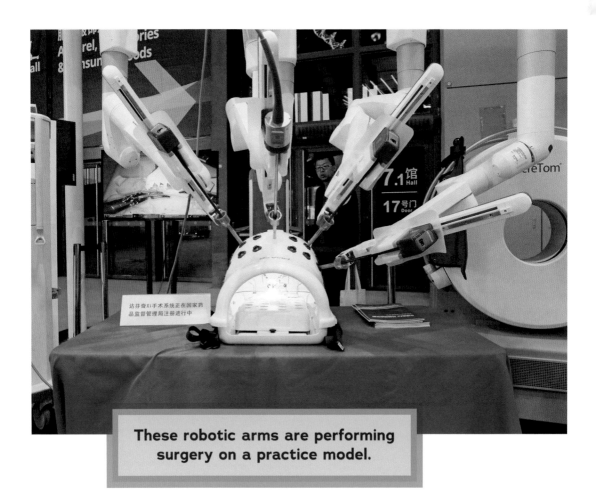

These robotic arms are performing surgery on a practice model.

Other robots assist doctors with difficult surgeries. Some robots learn how surgeons move their hands and wrists. Then the robots can copy the movements and help during an operation. A doctor might guide the robot with a remote control. Other times, doctors use robotic arms for tricky operations. The doctor looks at a screen to see inside the patient. She controls the robotic arm to operate.

Chapter 2

STOPPING DISEASES BEFORE THEY START

You might worry about getting a shot when you visit your doctor. But the shot keeps you from getting sick.

Germs are tiny living things that cause disease. Inside a shot is a vaccine made of dead or weak germs. These germs won't make you sick, but they get your body ready to fight. Your body's immune cells make chemicals called antibodies to attack the germs. Then, if you encounter these germs later, the antibodies will kill the germs before you get sick.

Vaccines have made many dangerous diseases much less common.

When the Ebola vaccine was ready, nurses worked to get as many people vaccinated as possible.

When a new disease appears, medical scientists make new vaccines. In 2014, a disease called Ebola spread through parts of Africa. Thousands of people got sick and died. Scientists worked hard to find a way to stop Ebola. In about one year, they made a vaccine that worked. When the threat of Ebola rises again, people can get vaccinated. That stops the disease from spreading.

Medical Breakthroughs in Action

Ah-choo! Each winter millions of people get sick with flu. The illness is hard to control with a vaccine because there are many types of flu viruses. Often different types of flu sicken people each year. That's why many vaccines are made to combat them. Scientists are trying to make a vaccine that can stop most types of flu viruses. If they succeed, getting a flu shot every year may be a thing of the past!

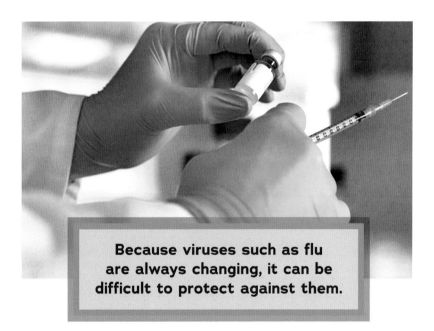

Because viruses such as flu are always changing, it can be difficult to protect against them.

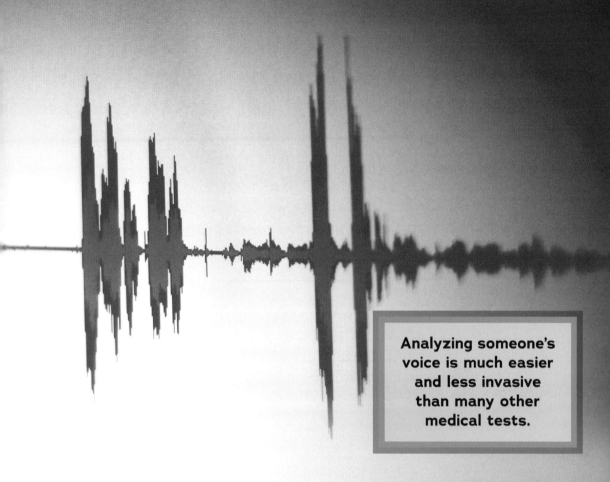

Analyzing someone's voice is much easier and less invasive than many other medical tests.

The Sound of Disease

Do you sound different when you are sick? You might not always be able to hear a difference. But computers can hear small changes in someone's voice. Scientists had people record their voices with a smartphone. Computers found certain sound patterns in the voices of people who were at risk of a heart attack. Learning more about these patterns could allow patients to get help before a heart attack occurs.

Scientists have found several illnesses that affect people's voices or the way they speak. In the future, someone who lives far from a doctor might send a voice recording from their computer or a smartphone. A computer could analyze the recording by searching for patterns associated with different illnesses. Then a doctor could see the patient remotely, diagnose diseases, and offer help.

With voice analysis, sick or elderly people wouldn't need to leave their homes to see a doctor.

Chapter 3

TREATING INJURIES AND CURING DISEASES

Many hospitals have 3D printer labs. Before surgery, a patient has X-rays taken. Doctors send the X-ray images to a 3D printer. The printer makes an exact 3D model of the patient's organs or bones. Then doctors can plan the surgery. They can even practice on the 3D model.

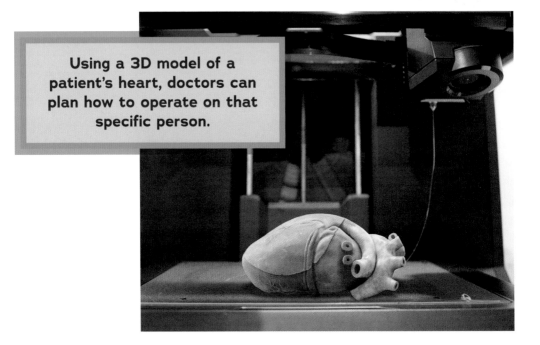

Using a 3D model of a patient's heart, doctors can plan how to operate on that specific person.

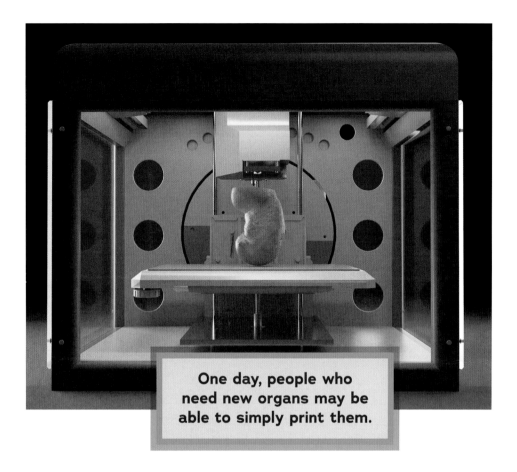

One day, people who need new organs may be able to simply print them.

Hospitals also use 3D printers to make surgical tools. A surgeon can design special tools for an operation. Then a 3D printer quickly prints them. The printed plastic tools are less expensive than steel.

Some 3D printers use bioink. They can print material that contains living cells. Researchers are experimenting with printing skin for burn victims. Someday doctors might print entire organs or other body parts.

For thousands of years, people made artificial limbs with iron or wood. They were heavy, difficult to use, and expensive. But 3D printers can print light, custom limbs made of plastic. Children who use artificial limbs must get new ones as they grow. A 3D printer makes this fast and affordable.

Many find 3D-printed limbs fit more comfortably than other artificial limbs.

Coding Spotlight

You don't have to be a doctor to print an artificial limb. A group of volunteers, e-NABLE, helps people who need an arm or hand. They use computer programs to design artificial hands and arms. The design software sends instructions to a 3D printer. The printer then lays down colorful plastic in layers to create the hand. So far, volunteers have printed about eighteen hundred hands for children.

Some of e-NABLE's hands are inspired by superheroes or movie characters.

By learning how frogs can regrow legs, scientists might find a way for humans to regrow limbs.

One day, people might even regrow fingers, toes, and lost limbs themselves. Scientists experimented on frogs that were missing legs. They used a 3D printer to make a special container called a bioreactor. The bioreactor held chemicals that made body tissue grow. The scientists attached the bioreactor to the frogs for one day. The frogs began to grow new legs!

Growing New Organs

Normally, humans can only grow new cells for hair, skin, and nails. We cannot grow most other kinds of cells. Could medical breakthroughs help people grow new organs?

Scientists can 3D-print noses like this one, but they are also beginning to grow them in labs.

Scientists are learning how to change skin cells into other types of cells. They placed a tiny device in the skin cells of mice and pigs. The device reprogrammed the skin cells so they grew into nerve cells. The scientists also made skin cells grow into blood vessels. One day, people with heart disease might use their own skin cells to grow a new heart. Someone with a brain injury could grow new nerve cells to repair it.

When skin cells become other cells, they change shape and size.

Science Fact or Science Fiction?

People can get new organs from pigs.

Not yet!

Someone with kidney disease might need a new kidney. But it's common for sick people to wait many years for a donated organ. Scientists are working on a surprising solution: getting organs from healthy pigs! Scientists try to change pig organs by replacing pig genes with human genes. That way a human body might be able to use a pig's organ. Scientists have successfully transplanted pig kidneys and hearts into monkeys. People could be next!

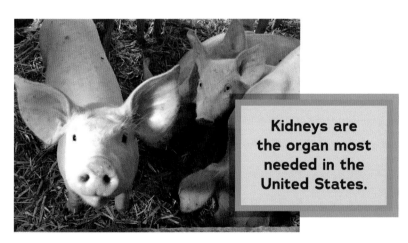

Kidneys are the organ most needed in the United States.

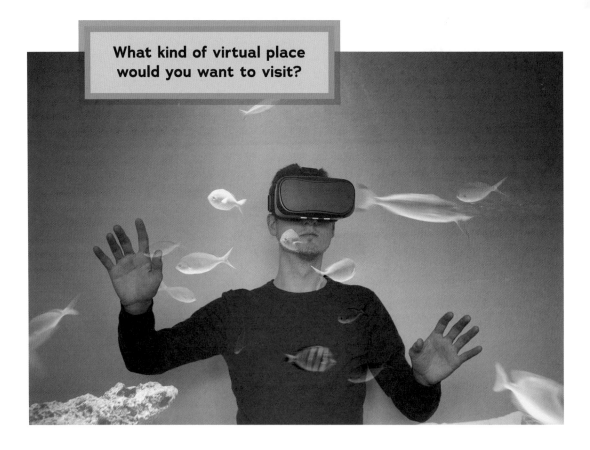

What kind of virtual place would you want to visit?

Virtual Reality

Sometimes pain-relief medicine has bad side effects. Doctors are experimenting with virtual reality headsets to relieve pain instead. The headsets make your brain think you are somewhere else. Imagine you have just broken your arm. You are in pain, so your doctor gives you a headset. You see coral reefs, and fish and dolphins swimming alongside you. Because you are distracted and having fun, you forget about your pain. Virtual reality could help people get better with less medicine.

Chapter 4

THE FUTURE OF MEDICINE

Every person's body is different. That's because we all have different genes. You get your genes from your biological parents. Genes tell your body how to work and grow. They can also affect how likely you are to get certain diseases.

The genes you get from your parents determine traits such as hair or eye color.

Many future medical research efforts will target the ways people's genes affect their health. Information from genes will help patients monitor themselves for certain diseases. Scientists will try to make treatments specific to each patient's genes.

A PATIENT'S GENES COULD TELL DOCTORS WHICH MEDICAL TREATMENTS WILL BE MOST EFFECTIVE.

Science Fact or Science Fiction?

A patient's own cells can fight cancer.

It's a fact!

A new treatment uses a patient's own immune cells to attack cancer. First, doctors filter the immune cells out of the patient's blood. Then they add a special gene to the cells. The gene lets the cells recognize the patient's cancer. The doctors grow millions of these new cells in a laboratory. Then they put the cells back in the patient's blood. The new gene sticks to cancer cells and kills them.

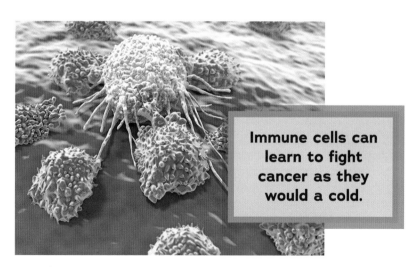

Immune cells can learn to fight cancer as they would a cold.

What if a blood test could find cancer before someone gets sick? Scientists learned that genetic material from cancer cells sticks to tiny gold particles. They made a blood test that uses these gold particles. Blood with cancer cells makes the particles turn a different color than blood with healthy cells. Researchers hope this test will be an early way to detect every kind of cancer.

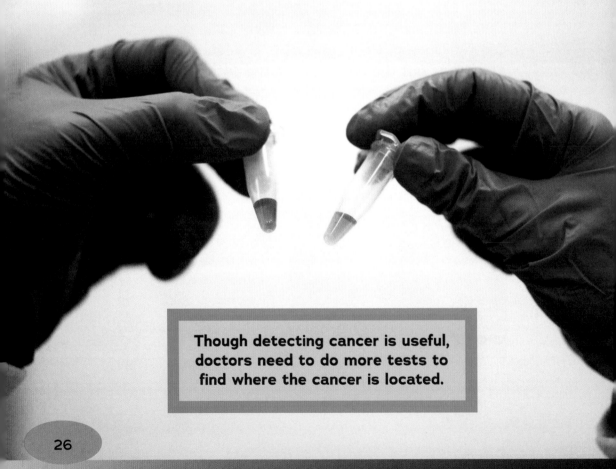

Though detecting cancer is useful, doctors need to do more tests to find where the cancer is located.

Tiny Trackers

Medical scientists also want to help people living with diseases such as diabetes. People with diabetes have trouble getting energy from food. They must check the level of glucose, a type of sugar, in their blood. To do this, they have to give themselves blood tests.

Many patients with diabetes must prick their fingers to draw blood.

Many diabetes patients don't like drawing their own blood. But there's another way to check glucose: tears. Scientists are making smart contact lenses with special sensors. These sensors will measure the glucose levels of the wearer's tears. If the glucose level drops or gets too high, the sensors will let the wearer know. Someday these contact lenses might be able to track other diseases too.

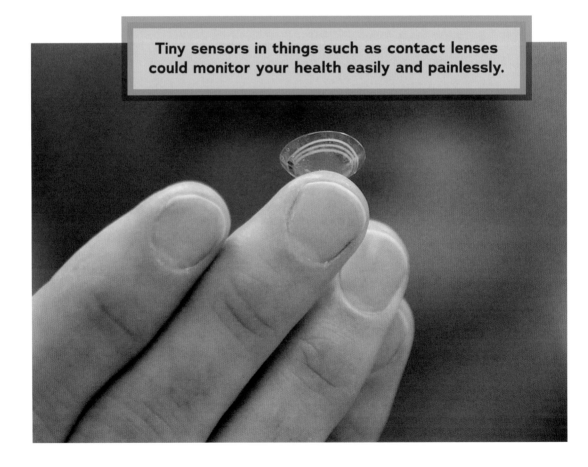

Tiny sensors in things such as contact lenses could monitor your health easily and painlessly.

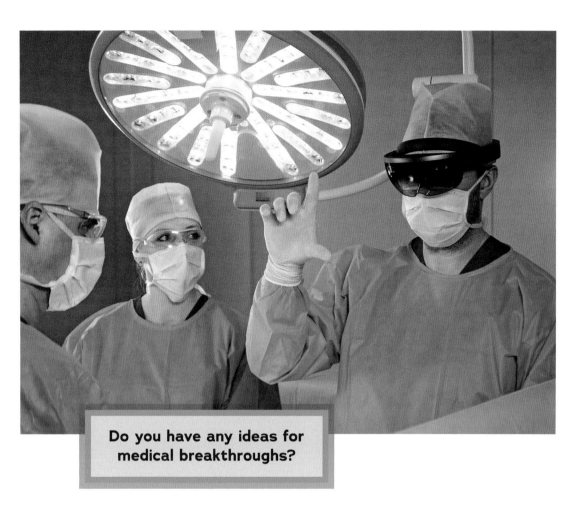

Do you have any ideas for medical breakthroughs?

Every day, medical scientists find new ways to improve human health. The next medical breakthrough could be something no one has imagined yet!

Glossary

antibody: a chemical your body makes to fight disease

bioink: a kind of ink a 3D printer uses to print living cells

bioreactor: a device that contains and grows living cells

cancer: a disease caused when cells divide without stopping and invade other cells

cell: a unit that makes up all plants and animals

diagnose: to identify an illness or medical condition

gene: a part of a cell parents pass to their offspring that contains instructions for cells

immune cell: a type of cell in the body that fights disease

sensor: a device that measures and responds to something

vaccine: a group of weak germs that helps the body prepare to fight a disease

virtual reality: a computer-generated image that you can interact with